Teen Guide to STARTING A BUSINESS

Tom Streissguth

San Diego, CA

For more information, contact:
ReferencePoint Press, Inc.
PO Box 27779
San Diego, CA 92198
www.ReferencePointPress.com

LIBRARY OF CONGRESS CATALOGING-IN-PUBLICATION DATA

Names: Streissguth, Thomas, 1958- author
Title: Teen guide to starting a business / by Tom Streissguth.
Description: San Diego, CA : ReferencePoint Press, Inc, 2026. | Includes bibliographical references and index.
Identifiers: LCCN 2025035347 (print) | LCCN 2025035348 (ebook) | ISBN 9781678212520 library binding | ISBN 9781678212537 ebook
Subjects: LCSH: New business enterprises--Management--Juvenile literature | Entrepreneurship--Juvenile literature | Success in business--Juvenile literature | Young businesspeople--Juvenile literature
Classification: LCC HD62.5 .S78 2026 (print) | LCC HD62.5 (ebook) | DDC 658.1/1--dc23/eng/20250912
LC record available at https://lccn.loc.gov/2025035347
LC ebook record available at https://lccn.loc.gov/2025035348

CONTENTS

What It Takes to Start a Business

There are many different kinds of successful new businesses. They come in all sizes, they serve all kinds of markets and locations, and they offer a wide range of products and services. Their owners and founders do have a few things in common, including persistence and belief in themselves. These traits are a strong part of their personal makeup and help them excel at business start-ups.

Giving Up Is Not an Option

One of these natural entrepreneurs is Dan Lok. When he was sixteen, Lok ran into some rough times. His parents had separated, although his father was providing his mother with financial support. His father then declared bankruptcy when the family business failed. He could no longer send money to help Lok or his mom. Seeing a look of hopelessness and fear on his mother's face, Lok realized he now had to be the breadwinner.

> "I couldn't afford to quit—and if you don't quit, then you can't fail."[1]
>
> —Dan Lok, founder of an advertising agency

Ordinary jobs paying minimum wage didn't work out. Lok had a hard time following instructions from the boss. So he started his own business. When that didn't make money, he started another. He started a vending machine company, tried delivery services, and became a stock trader. In all, he tried thirteen different ventures. All of them failed. "I never gave up," he told an interviewer. "Because I couldn't afford to quit—and if you don't quit, then you can't fail."[1]

Then Lok met Alan Jacques, a leader in the field of marketing and advertising. While attending one of Jacques's marketing seminars, Lok believed he had found the answer to his long quest. He bought Jacques lunch, then started working around his teacher's office, asking questions and doing odd jobs. Lok learned a lot from his mentor and tried to imitate his success.

One day, he set himself a simple task: writing a sales letter. Jacques gave him some advice: try again. Lok rewrote the letter a total of seven times. Finally, Jacques agreed to help Lok start an advertising agency. Lok felt he had finally found his niche. Within a year, his sales letters were generating serious money. The hard times were over.

Believing in Yourself

Of course, it's not always enough to have the right personality. Like Dan Lok, Jesse Kemmerer also had a business vision and a lot of belief in himself. When he was a freshman in high school, he started teaching himself website design. He believed he was good enough to offer this service to local businesses.

Meeting with potential clients can be an important first step in launching your own business.

Kemmerer knew that projecting confidence was a big ingredient in business success. Not only is confidence required, so is the ability to handle "no" and move on. He made a lot of sales calls and heard a lot of rejections. But a few business owners did agree to meet him in person.

Kemmerer landed a few jobs. He found that some business owners were willing to take a chance and hire him. He was young and confident, after all. He seemed to know what he was talking about. He charged a reasonable amount. He could see a bright future ahead, and he started planning for the good life. "I was going to be a success story, and an all the more impressive one because of my age," Kemmerer wrote in a blog account of his early career. "I was wrong."[2]

Hard but Valuable Lessons

Kemmerer discovered that in any service business, making a sale is just the start of a business relationship. Website designers, for example, do more than sell a product. They have to deliver a service, and the service has to be so good that the client won't just hire someone else. For Kemmerer, that meant building and maintaining cutting edge websites that bring in page views and customers.

> "No matter what business you're in, ask yourself if you can deliver."[3]
>
> —Jesse Kemmerer, founder of a website development business

Kemmerer's websites were okay, but not great. Some of them didn't function well, and some stopped working altogether. He stopped making sales calls, and then stopped answering the phone. "No matter what business you're in," he recalls, "ask yourself if you can deliver. If you sell a product, is that product the best it could be? Does your customer get out of it what you promise? If you perform a service, are you truly competent at that service, or are you just good for your age?"[3]

Kemmerer was good, but not great. He was bright and confident, but he had a hard time leveling up to great websites and great customer service. So the business slowed and then closed. It was a hard lesson, but a valuable one.

Eventually, he got back to work and rebuilt Local Sight, his web development business. He had learned a few things along the way. Lesson one: It takes a lot more than confidence to start a business. There are other ingredients that are just as important but are harder to perceive. The way to learn them is to take the necessary risk and build something. You might fail—you'll probably fail—but surviving and learning from that failure can build something that lasts.

CHAPTER ONE

Just Starting Out

Business starts with an idea. Someone makes a suggestion, or a few friends kick around a moneymaking concept. Then comes a plan. That idea just might work, but how? If the concept can support a business, the answer will come. But the hard work has just begun.

Nathanael Farrelly had just started his nursing career, but he was already beginning to burn out. His job in a busy hospital demanded an early start and long hours. "I remember waking up every morning . . . just sick to my stomach," he told an interviewer from the business channel CNBC. "That start really opened up a lot of anxiety and stress."[4]

But while on the job he discovered a new way of delivering health care to hospital patients. "Infusion therapy" allowed them to get essential drugs and treatment at home. A nurse still needed to administer medications. But the nurse could work freelance, through an agency. The nurse could accept a little work or a lot and could keep flexible hours.

Farrelly hit on an idea for his own business. He called it Revitalized Specialty Infusion, a job agency for infusion nursing. It would help find nurses for patients who needed them. It would also allow nurses to work on their own schedule. Revitalized Specialty Infusion turned out to be a smart idea. When the COVID-19 pandemic hit in 2020, demand for at-home nursing boomed. The business had no trouble finding clients and caretakers for them, and it was soon thriving.

Finding the Idea

Revitalized began with an inspiration on the job. Like Farrelly, many entrepreneurs—people who create and run their own businesses—simply see a need. They produce something new or offer a service to meet that need. Many rely on their own interests and talents, while some draw on their work experiences. Then they apply hard work and enthusiasm, which are essential to the success of any new business.

An important step along this path is to get a feel for the market. Entrepreneurs use many different resources to understand who would buy their products or use their services. This means knowing the age of typical customers, where they live and work, and how much money they would be willing to spend for what the business has to offer.

There are different ways to figure this out. You might be really good at fixing Model Ts from the 1920s, but not many people own one-hundred-year-old cars. It might be a good idea to show up at some antique car shows and talk to owners. They might have cars from different eras, each with their own mechanical issues and problems. There might be some future clients in attendance.

It may be a little early to think about marketing, but now is the time to understand who, where, and who your customers are. Some entrepreneurs started out with only their family and friends as their market. From a small beginning, they grew the business and turned it into a profitable success.

In order to gauge the market, many start-up companies do surveys and focus groups and carry out research on demographics and market trends. But there are easier ways to do customer research. It can be done by simply talking to people to find out what they need and want. Friends, family, teachers, neighbors, students, and coworkers may be willing to share their thoughts. They may offer new ideas on just what the marketplace is seeking.

Family, Friends, and Neighbors

It's possible to do some research in your own home. When he was fourteen years old, Fonzi Coleman came up with an idea to make candles by using handmade, reusable concrete molds. It

> **"Don't wait to be older—just start with what you have and keep going."[5]**
>
> —Fonzi Coleman, Bubbles and Blaze founder

was a simple project meant to create something his mom could use in the house. The project turned into Bubbles and Blaze, a business that sells a variety of scented, eco-friendly candles across the country. Coleman offered this advice to an interviewer: "Don't wait to be older—just start with what you have and keep going."[5]

Neighbors can also offer good insights. They may have dogs that need walking, a lawn that needs mowing, or snow that needs to be shoveled. Their car could use a wash, or they wouldn't mind someone taking some garage clutter off their hands. There's one way to find out—seek them out and ask questions. They may even have some business experience of their own and have some ideas on how a new enterprise can get off the ground and succeed.

A family loads their van with goods before heading off to work at the local farmer's market. Many large businesses have small roots, starting with just family and friends.

Structuring a Business

There's no law stopping teenagers from running a business. But there's more to it than making and selling things. Anyone with a business has to decide what kind of company they want to run. There are several different legal structures available.

Many under-eighteen entrepreneurs form sole proprietorships. With a sole proprietorship, the business belongs to an individual, and there are no partners or corporate structure. The owner earns the income and is responsible for paying any taxes the business owes. A young owner can also appoint a parent or guardian as a trustee to handle tax and legal matters.

Once a person turns eighteen, they can sign legal contracts. They also may file papers to incorporate their own company. The most common form of corporation is a limited liability corporation, or LLC. Income and assets belong to the business, not the individual owner.

Business owners establish an LLC by filing paperwork with a state agency. They pay a fee, register a business name, and write articles of organization. They also appoint registered agents who can accept legal paperwork on their behalf. One last step is to get a tax identification number from the Internal Revenue Service. Every year, the LLC has to report its income and pay taxes.

Networking with others to determine their needs and their problems is a key part of any start-up business. An entrepreneur can network in many different ways. It could be an informal occasion such as a wedding, a backyard barbeque, or a sports event. It could be a store opening or a job fair.

Networking is all about meeting people, asking and answering questions, and discovering solvable problems. "I hardly ever leave a conversation where I'm not spreading the word on 'hey, this is what I'm doing,'"[6] says April Wilkerson, who runs Wilker Do's, which sells useful do-it-yourself projects and materials. It may seem tough for a kid still in school to mix in the business world, but networking on any level can help a business thrive.

Of course, being young is no barrier to starting a company. Many business owners started out before age eighteen. "In fact, being a teenager is one of the best stages of life to start a business in," says Jake Butler in his book *Teen Entrepreneur: The Dream*.

> "Being a teenager is one of the best stages of life to start a business in."[7]
>
> —Jake Butler, author of *Teen Entrepreneur: The Dream*

"The earlier you start, the earlier you can reap the rewards." Butler also points out that teenagers have "a stronger connection to youth culture, social media, and the general pulse of the times than adults."[7] This gives them a real advantage in the task of building a new business.

Seeing a Need

Rayhan Khimji started Snacc in his native India at age sixteen. Many kids he knew didn't eat well. They were busy with classes and sports and didn't have the time or the interest to learn about good nutrition. Khimji, a martial arts competitor, was used to overcoming challenges. He saw this particular problem as one he could try to solve. So he created a healthy, tasty protein bar.

This wasn't an ordinary protein bar marketed to adults. Instead, Khimji targeted customers like him: active teenagers. In advertising and on social media, he described his product as suitable for younger people. This was deliberate: Like many new business owners, he was searching for a niche—a small slice of a much bigger market where his company could find customers and thrive.

It's important when starting a business to think about your niche. It may be a long and difficult search, and one that takes some unexpected turns even after the business gets off the ground. "I saw a glaring gap," Khimji told an interviewer from *Youth Incorporated*, an online education, business and lifestyle magazine created in India for teens. "There were no healthy, tasty snacks that were convenient to take to school or to sporting events. In school, there were no alternatives to chips or pizza and home-packed lunches would always get cold and stale by afternoon . . . so I sat down and did some brainstorming."[8]

Picking a Business Model

Entrepreneurs like Rayhan Khimji use their own talents and energy to build a new business. They can also benefit from the experience of others. Someone may have already built a business

Youth is no barrier to starting a business. Many business owners have gotten their start before age eighteen.

similar to the one you're thinking of. They've already got a template or business model that they use. This is a concept of how to offer products and run the business that's already been tested and proved to succeed.

Business models come in many forms and sizes. There are a few important steps in selecting the right one. The entrepreneur has to identify the products or services to sell, the target market, and the best way to sell to that market. One business model might be perfect for selling clothes online, for example, but the same model might not work at all for a new tutoring agency.

Once a business is up and running, the owner can evaluate how well the model is working. There are no rules or laws involved—entrepreneurs are in charge of handling the business model. They can make adjustments in the model depending on how well it's working or how the market is changing.

One of the simplest models is the retail business. A retailer buys goods from manufacturers or wholesalers, and then marks up the price to sell those goods to customers. Some retailers use online sites, some sell from physical stores, and some do both.

Another common business model is fee-for-service. In this model, an expert skill or specialty is offered to the public for a fixed price or some kind of time rate; by the hour, for example. Lawn service, DJing, tutoring, computer repair, and car detailing are all fee-for-service businesses.

A marketplace business, such as Amazon, offers a platform online for many different people or businesses to offer their goods and services. An affiliate business earns money by promoting products on behalf of other companies. Affiliate marketing is big on the internet, where influencers on Instagram and other social media earn money by promoting new products.

Subscription businesses, such as Spotify or Netflix, offer a service for a monthly fee. Many of these companies bring in new customers by offering a basic, stripped-down version of their service for free, then offering enhanced content for a premium. This is known as the freemium model. Subscriptions bring an important advantage known as recurring revenue. This is money that arrives from customers (or members) on a regular basis. Recurring revenue makes it easier to manage a business and plan for the future.

Networking Online

Meeting potential customers and learning from experienced business owners will help most anyone who wants to create a new business. There are many ways to mingle with other business owners and experienced entrepreneurs—especially online. LinkedIn is an online meeting place where millions of business owners post profiles and talk about their work. It's a good place to announce product launches, partnerships, and company milestones.

Networking events abound in most big cities. "Speed networking" takes a cue from speed dating: people meet, chat for a few minutes, and trade business cards. A local chamber of commerce will have a calendar of events. These organizations specialize in helping businesses. They run conferences and hold regular meetings. They offer advice, provide guidance on laws and licensing, and can direct entrepreneurs to mentors and business specialists.

In fee-for-service business models, such as tutoring, specialty services are offered at a fixed price or hourly rate.

Having the right business model in place helps a business thrive. An entrepreneur can ask for guidance from someone who's already operated this kind of business. A familiar model makes it easier for a start-up entrepreneur to explain a new business to investors. It gives partners and employees a solid idea of their role in the company. A business model also makes it easier for customers to understand the business. They may have dealt with another company that operates in the same way, so they're comfortable in considering a similar company, even a new competitor.

Of course, entrepreneurs sometimes come up with entirely new business models. Usually this happens after they consider the competition and figure out an even better way to get clients and serve the market. This is the kind of breakthrough that builds successful companies, even new industries. As experienced entrepreneurs have realized, in business anything is possible.

Making a Plan

For a young entrepreneur planning a start-up, there are many different types of businesses to choose from. Some will demand long hours, others will take less time. Some can be done entirely online. Others call for a special skill or talent or a lot of space to operate. Many—not all—require a large investment of money.

You might know all about design, production, or marketing. That doesn't mean you know how to run a business—at least not yet. That's a different talent, and one not everyone is good at. Many people starting businesses have little or no idea of the problems to solve or the hurdles they'll have to overcome.

"Directing our actions to the improvement of someone or something outside ourselves motivates us to succeed."[9]

—Chris Vanderzyden, author of *A–Z Blueprint for Success*

A key factor in making a new business work is motivation and doing what you love to do. If you're not sure what you love to do, Chris Vanderzyden, in her book *A–Z Blueprint for Success*, offers a clue: "Directing our actions to the improvement of someone or something outside ourselves motivates us to succeed."[9]

Seeking Wisdom

Anyone who starts out in business soon discovers there's one thing they will never lack: advice. Library and bookstore shelves are groaning under the weight of books telling you how, when, where, and why to run a business. There are YouTube videos on very specific business problems, and there are classes, seminars, and mentorship groups.

"If you do the things that are easier first, then you can actually make a lot of progress."[10]

—Mark Zuckerberg, cofounder of Facebook

In fact, there's a lot of good business advice available, and from all kinds of people. Mark Zuckerberg, for example, encourages entrepreneurs just starting out to take it slow. The cofounder of Facebook wrote, "I think a simple rule of business is, if you do the things that are easier first, then you can actually make a lot of progress."[10] Zuckerberg built Facebook from a simple concept he dreamed up in college: putting a student directory online. He started out by doing something that, for him, was easy and fun.

It's also smart to speak to people who've already been there. If they run a business in a similar field, they'll know about problems and opportunities that will come up. Seeking out business grants, or contacting potential lenders or partners, are also good ideas. Whether or not these contacts play a role in your business, they might be able to offer good advice. But first, they will probably want to see your business plan.

Mark Zuckerberg has built Facebook from a simple concept to one of the world's most successful businesses.

Putting a Plan Together

A business plan begins with a mission statement. It can be a paragraph or a sentence or two. The mission statement sets out in a few words the purpose and goal of the company.

Good mission statements aren't complicated. They're easy to understand and remember. Some huge companies have very simple ones. Google's mission statement is "To organize the world's information and make it universally accessible and useful." For Starbucks: "To inspire and nurture the human spirit—one person, one cup and one neighborhood at a time." For Walmart: "We save people money so they can live better."[11]

Following the mission statement is a summary of the plan. Here all the details in the plan are boiled down to short bites of information. The summary gives the name of the company, a brief history, the business goals, and a description of the products the company will make or the services it will provide.

The summary also explains who the customers are. It gives the names and experience of the owner and any partners. A summary also has a bottom line: how much the business will need to get up and running and where the money will come from.

More Fine Details

After the summary, the business plan describes the industry the business will belong to. This part of the plan should answer a few important questions. Is this kind of business needed? Is the need growing? What are its future opportunities?

The plan should describe the products or services the business will offer. If it's a subscription business, for example, the plan will detail the monthly fees customers will pay. If a free tier of service is offered, that should be included. Or if rates vary, that too belongs in the plan.

If the business will offer products, then the plan should provide a description of these offerings. It should also detail how customers will purchase the goods and how the business will

Insurance

Insurance may be the last thing on the mind of an eager entrepreneur. But buying business insurance is a way of covering all bases and protecting a young company. Without it, a business owner can face some serious financial issues.

This kind of insurance protects a business from liability claims. As soon as your business opens its doors, an unhappy customer or client can sue for damages. This can include injury or a financial loss. They can ask a court to find your business liable and order your business to pay. If your business is a sole proprietorship or simple partnership, you can be personally liable for any damages.

Business insurance will protect against liability claims, up to a certain amount. The expense depends on what type of business you have, and the dollar limits on protection. The insurance may also protect against any loss, damage to, or theft of your property. Some businesses, such as health care providers, are legally required to carry liability insurance.

deliver them. If it's an online business, the plan should feature a sample product page, showing exactly what the customers see when they log on to search the inventory.

The plan should next describe the market for the product. That means considering age, gender, location, education, and income to identify the potential customer base. Also worth considering is whether this is something people would buy every day, once in a while, or seasonally. The plan should also describe how the business will get the product to the customers: through retail outlets, online selling, mail order, wholesalers, or any other channel.

Marketing and Money

The plan will have to include details on how the business will market itself. This includes finding the target market, advertising to that market, and setting up social media accounts such as Facebook or Instagram. Important aspects of marketing, such as how the business will handle orders and returns, should be described in this section of the plan.

Along with a marketing plan, a business plan should also reveal start-up finances. Of course, the business will need money to function. Start-up capital is all the money needed to get a business up and running until it begins to make a profit. A business plan needs to show the expenses, which could be rent, equipment, raw materials, insurance, licenses, salaries, and utilities, among other things. Expenses have a way of coming up unexpectedly, and costs constantly increase. To show this is a serious business and not just a dream, a smart entrepreneur needs to anticipate as many of those costs as possible.

But where will the start-up capital come from? Financing is a key challenge for any new business. A bank may lend money to a reliable borrower. The federal government makes loans available through the Small Business Administration. A nonprofit or a development organization seeking to encourage new business activity may offer grants of money. With a business plan in hand, an entrepreneur may also seek partners or private investors. The business owner offers a share of the company and its profits to people or firms that agree to provide capital.

And then there's bootstrapping, which means using your own money to finance a new business. Some entrepreneurs rely on personal savings. They may also have family members or friends who are willing to help. Bootstrapping is risky. If the business fails, it's your money (or money from family and friends) that is lost. But it can also lead to success.

Diving In to a New Business

Bunim Laskin used his own money to start a pool-rental company. He came up with the idea while working for a pool maintenance company. What he noticed is that almost everyone loves pools, but not everyone has one. So why not connect pool owners with people having parties and groups or families just seeking a fun afternoon? His business model was the peer-to-peer rental business, such as Airbnb, which connects homeowners with vacationers who want a nice, non-hotel place to stay.

Laskin's business Swimply was underway. "I knocked on doors, collected availabilities, and handled bookings over the

The company Swimply, which started out as a pool-rental service, is a bootstrapping success story. Originally funded by its owner, the company expanded quickly into a booming business.

phone," he explains about the early days. "Even with that rudimentary process, it went viral locally."[12] Swimply expanded from swimming pools to tennis courts, basketball and pickleball courts, and eventually entire homes. His company signed up hosts in dozens of cities in the United States, Canada, and Australia.

What's Your Name?

No matter how it's financed, a new business has some legal details to cover before opening day. First, the entrepreneur has to come up with a name for the business. Whatever it is, the name should be easy to remember and give a clue to what the business does.

There are some legal restrictions on names. The name for your new business cannot be identical to a name already in use. Nor can it be so similar to another company's name that it causes confusion. A name can't be an imitation of an official government agency. It wouldn't be legal, for example, to call a new business "Department of Revenue" or "Sheriff's Department."

Going the Franchise Route

It's not necessary to have a brilliant new product or service of one's own. An entrepreneur can simply buy into a proven business. A turnkey business is already up and running and is purchased by a new owner. Franchising is another way to go.

A franchise already has the brand, the product line, the store concept, and the marketing. The entrepreneur simply pays a fee to the parent company and opens their own location. They also pay a percentage of their sales to the parent company.

McDonald's and Chili's are big-name franchise restaurants. Dunkin' and Cinnabon, often spotted at the mall, are franchises. Smaller franchises include car washes, fitness gyms, and laundromats. Some don't require a physical location. Franchise businesses that can be operated out of a work van include windshield repair, carpet cleaning. landscaping, and swimming pool maintenance.

Franchises support a new business with a familiar brand name, which tends to attract customers. But there is a financial hurdle to overcome. The franchisor needs money for the franchise fee, materials, inventory, and other costs. The franchise contract also sets a percentage of sales that must be paid to the parent company.

In most states, the office of the secretary of state registers names and issues business licenses. This agency will have a searchable list of business names currently in use. If the name you've selected is not going to be legal, the site will let you know, and you won't be able to register or protect the name.

Do You Need a License?

The secretary of state will also have information on what licenses your type of business will need. Licensing can be a confusing patchwork. Some states or cities will require a license, while others may not require a license at all. This may figure in the decision on location. Health care providers, food businesses, accounting services, retail stores, cosmetologists, building contractors, and electricians are some of the businesses that will need a license.

Eight-year-old Asa Baker found out about licenses on a hot summer afternoon in 2022. Her lemonade was selling, and her customers at the Alliance Rib and Food Festival, in Alliance, Ohio, were happy. Then a police officer arrived and asked for her food vendor permit. She didn't have one. Her stand was forced to close, briefly. Once she paid for the permit, her stand was up and running again, and selling snacks as well. In the next few weeks, in fact, publicity about the incident boosted her sales, and she even opened a new location. But Asa had learned a good lesson about starting a business—any business.

Permits and More

Asa's lemonade stand was a temporary structure. But if your business has a permanent physical location, you also may need a building permit, a fire permit, and a zoning permit. Even if it's just a storefront that you rent, you'll need some kind of certificate allowing you to operate a business there.

It's also a good idea to register a business. This is also done with the secretary of state's office. It's a way of recording your business name and operating with some legal protections. Your

Temporary structures, like this California food truck for dog treats, do not require expensive building permits. They may, however, require licenses and other types of permits.

state may not allow anyone under age eighteen to register a business. If you're younger, you need a trustee, parent, or guardian to carry out this step and to represent you in any legal matter.

Some businesses also need a state or federal tax ID number. Other business owners file taxes as individuals and just use their Social Security numbers for paying taxes. Business lawyers and accountants are trained to take care of these details. For most people, getting all this paperwork squared away is not the most fun part of running a business. But no matter who gets it done, it's all necessary to get your enterprise up and running. And it's smart to put things in order so problems don't come up in the future.

CHAPTER THREE

Getting to Opening Day

After much planning and preparation, opening day will arrive. The business gets underway, welcomes its first customers and, if all goes well, makes its first sales. This is the day entrepreneurs have worked for and dreamed of, while making decisions that will contribute to their success or failure.

For a brick-and-mortar business that relies on customer visits, one of the most important decisions is location. For a restaurant or shop, visibility is crucial. The heavier the volume of traffic past the business, the better the chance of attracting customers and making sales. There is a downside to a high-traffic location, however. It can be more expensive to rent, because it has more value for business owners.

Some types of businesses can be set up in a private home. Owners mark off areas used to assemble products or to package goods for shipment. There may be an area for computers, printers, and desks. There may be a photo or video studio or a kitchen. There are hundreds of different types of home-based businesses; for example, jewelry makers, fashion studios, barber shops, toy makers, eBay and Amazon sellers, and antique radio traders.

A home-based business saves money and works well for entrepreneurs until it doesn't. Typically, a home-based business reaches a moment when it grows too large and busy to fit into a single room. At that point it might be time to look for a location that better suits a growing business.

Opening day is an exciting milestone for a new business owner. It's a great opportunity to introduce yourself and your business to the public.

For some businesses, physical location is less important than an online presence. Some successful businesses operate strictly online, but nearly all businesses have at least a web page where the public can make contact, learn about the business, explore products and services, and meet management and employees. Developing a presence on social media, such as Facebook, X, and Instagram, can help a business reach a broader market. Linking to other companies on these sites is a great way to develop leads that can bring inquiries and sales.

Setting the Hours

New business owners will also have to set business hours so that customers know exactly when the business will be open. Customers should be able to make contact easily—either in person or by phone or email. And the business should respond quickly to any questions.

Of course, there's a lot to do outside of business hours. For most entrepreneurs, operating a business means more than full-time hours. There are decisions to make and things to take care of every day, all day long. Anyone who is thinking about starting a business has to consider how much time they have available and how much time they're willing to spend on managing and growing the business. Many entrepreneurs step back after realizing their business needs more time and energy than they have available.

This is where research comes in handy for a new business owner. It's useful to find an entrepreneur in the same or a very similar line of work. They might not want to reveal details of their operation. But they might be willing to share their views on what's required in terms of time, money, materials, energy, and outside help.

Making connections like this can be challenging. But mingling with people is a necessary business skill. "We always tell kids, don't talk to strangers," entrepreneur Brian Weisfeld, who helped build the IMAX theater business, told an interviewer. "But ultimately, you've got to learn how and to look people in the eye and to get comfortable with failure, and people saying no and taking risks and all those wonderful things."[13]

"We always tell kids, don't talk to strangers. But ultimately, you've got to learn how."[13]

—Brian Weisfeld, entrepreneur

Up and Running

All of this preparation is leading to that all-important moment: the first day of business. The date should be chosen with care. Tutors, for example, might want to start just before a fall or winter school term gets underway. Crafters and toy makers should have products ready after Halloween, when the holiday shopping season begins. Wedding planners should open up in the spring, which is a popular time for weddings. This is also a good season for landscapers to get a new business going.

Opening day gives a business owner a great opportunity to promote the business to the public. Throwing a good opening day party could mean free publicity if the event attracts the attention of local media. The online platform Shopify also advises that opening day is a good time to "reward early followers and supporters. Choosing

Zoning Laws

Business owners who rely on a physical store or workshop or use a factory or warehouse have to think about zoning. Most cities and counties have zoning laws, which dictate how property in certain areas can be used. Some neighborhoods might be strictly residential, for example. Others might allow factories or restaurants and retail stores. Cities can also reserve open spaces, wetlands, or forests for public use.

Zoning laws can also apply to small businesses that operate out of a home. If a place of business is open to the public, it may have to be in a commercial zone. This may also go for a business that makes or takes deliveries. On top of zoning laws, many neighborhood associations limit commercial businesses within their boundaries. Some even restrict garage sales or lemonade stands.

A city planning department is usually the contact to find out about zoning. It will have a detailed map and an explanation of how your neighborhood and town are zoned.

to host an exclusive event or offer a promotion to your pre-launch subscribers is a way to reward them for betting on you early."[14]

Opening day is a good time to focus on your target market. A kid-focused business, such as a toy shop, can offer a scavenger hunt, games, or a photo contest. Barbecues and outdoor tables will attract a curious, hungry crowd. Live music will draw people, as will free samples and gift bags. Many businesses will also offer a celebrity or VIP guest, who mingles with arrivals, signs autographs, chats up the business, and poses for selfies. Having a VIP interact with the product builds excitement, as do free samples, a product demonstration, or coupons for discounts.

> "Choosing to host an exclusive event or offer a promotion to your pre-launch subscribers is a way to reward them for betting on you early."[14]
>
> —Shopify

Before a big event like this, it's good to do a soft launch. This is a practice run with a smaller, private crowd of family, friends, partners, and vendors—anyone involved somehow with the business. This is a chance to get feedback and ideas for opening day.

A buildup on social media is another key to opening day success. Advertising the event on a website, Facebook page, TikTok, or Instagram well in advance is a smart way to get people talking about it. A press release to a local newspaper might find its way into a small article that circulates to thousands of households.

Build a Following

Online communication is essential. Many of your future customers are spending hours of their day online. To reach them directly, it's necessary to collect email addresses and set up an email program. On a weekly or monthly schedule, the program can shoot them new information, promotions, business news, merchandise offerings, and whatever the business wants to announce. Software that can assemble and launch email blasts makes this task easy.

The business website also can run a countdown page. The page gives the number of days, hours, and minutes until your enterprise opens. A launch or countdown page is also a good way to collect email addresses from those who send a question to your business. Email lists can be purchased as well. Vendors

Online communication is essential for any business. Regular email outreach can be a key to success.

break down the potential customers by zip code, age, profession, and many other categories. Mailing lists do the same. Sending out flyers by regular mail is old-fashioned, but it can work to develop a base of customers.

User-generated content has also become a major ingredient in business marketing. Businesses gather this content by inviting customers to leave reviews or testimonials on products or services. A glowing review featured prominently on a website can be more effective than the promotional copy offered by the business. Photos of ordinary people using a product or sampling a menu offering are powerful.

Marketing

Arranging opening day fun for customers is one great way to market a business. It checks several important boxes for the business owner: attracting new customers, linking up with sponsors, engaging the community, and getting feedback in the early days. To pull off any event or promotion successfully, it's important to keep these and other marketing principles in mind.

The definition of marketing is pretty simple. It includes all the things a business does to communicate with its customers, current and future. There are many channels available for this, with some more useful and effective than others. It can take time and money to do well. But an entrepreneur can't ignore marketing. Without it, a new business will struggle to generate sales, because few people will know about it.

Traditional forms of marketing a small business, such as print ads in newspapers and magazines and mailing of flyers, still work, but the internet has created many more options for promoting a business. Large websites need ad revenue in some form to sustain themselves. So Google provides links that connect potential customers to a business through search results. Facebook sells a variety of advertising features, as do Amazon, YouTube, and Pinterest. Information about a business can be sent out with regular emails or with social media such as Facebook, Instagram, X, and TikTok.

Two Brands Are Sometimes Better than One

If a business finds its products gaining steady customers, it might consider partnership with a larger company. A food truck that is working well on a downtown corner may join up with an established restaurant. This is called co-branding. With co-branding, the truck would offer both its own and the restaurant's most popular entrées and sides. The truck could also try partnerships with small, home-based food producers. Their appetizers or desserts would then appear on the truck's menu. This boosts its appeal to a hungry public that always wants more choices.

Co-branding is very trendy among big consumer companies. Nike and Apple promote each other's products. FritoLay has joined up with Taco Bell, as have GoPro and Red Bull. But even a little start-up can benefit from a partnership with a local company. A lawn service, for example, can advertise its use of products from a nearby family hardware store. In exchange, the store can post news of a new customer discount for mowing, landscaping, or other outdoorsy services. It takes a little hustle, but if both companies can share advertising and promotion costs and grow their sales, it's a win-win.

Advertising is costly, however. For a small or start-up business, direct-response marketing can be much easier, as well as less costly and more effective. Direct response marketing means getting customers involved right away. This can be done through surveys, for example, or getting people to sign up for regular emails. An essential part of this effort is a website that promotes products, carries on transactions, and provides customer services and an email point of contact. For businesses that are carried out entirely online, this type of marketing is the best way to do business. "Direct response marketing is designed to evoke an immediate response," explains Allan Dib in *The 1-Page Marketing Plan*. "Such as opting in to your e-mail list, picking up the phone and calling for more information, placing an order or being directed to a web page."[15]

Solving the Online Study Problem

Web-based businesses now have a variety of tools they can use to engage customers. Many of these tools rely on artificial intelligence (AI), which is software that imitates human learning and decision-making. An AI program can help business owners develop detailed knowledge of the individuals who make up their market. AI can also be used to develop new products.

For Esan Durrani, there was much more to classes than a teacher and a chalkboard. He noticed that a class in English, for example, could offer knowledge in many different forms: books, notes, lectures, flash cards, and so on. But Durrani was frustrated by poorly organized online study sites. He saw possibilities for new kinds of online classroom tools, generated by the student's own books and assignments. And then he created his own company to fill the gap.

Durrani's website is called StudyFetch. Student users upload their own class materials, including lecture notes, study guides, recordings, and slides. The website then uses AI to build a set of materials that help the student master the subject. It might create flash cards, practice quizzes, or useful notes from the mountain of

Social media sites give businesses a way to connect with their customers. This small business owner is demonstrating her product's new "green" packaging.

course material, or even give advice on how to improve the writing and flow of essays submitted by the student. Using artificial intelligence tools, it functions through a conversational online tutor that responds to the student's own learning style. And it communicates in more than twenty different languages.

Generating Revenue

StudyFetch was "designed to add value to the resources provided by educators," Durrani explains on *Education Technology Insights*. "The platform serves as a supplement to teachers, not a replacement."[16] Durrani has attracted more than 1 million student users since he started his company in 2023. But how does an online business like this one earn money?

Unlike online businesses that sell physical products (such as clothing or jewelry), strictly digital businesses like StudyFetch have to figure out ways to generate revenue from the online services they offer. A website owner can restrict content to subscribers, who pay a monthly fee to access the material kept behind a paywall. The website can also run advertising. Companies will pay for banner or pop-up ads depending on how much traffic the website gets. Ads can also run on newsletters that go out to an email list, generated by those who sign up for any services the site provides. The website can also ask for donations.

StudyFetch used the premium subscription model. Users can access more features and higher data limits by paying a monthly fee. To encourage sign-ups, the site offers a free trial of these premium features. The trial period allows a user to sample the tools before deciding whether or not to pay for them.

Choosing a business model is just one of many decisions start-up entrepreneurs have to make. There are many others, big and small, important and trivial. The many tasks and choices facing a business owner, especially at the start, make it important to get a business plan down in some form. The plan serves not just to promote the company to investors, but to give the entrepreneur a framework for the long and tough business campaign ahead.

CHAPTER FOUR

What Comes Next

The first few months running a new business can be tough. It takes time to reach customers and convince them that they want or need your company's products or services. It's also a major project for any business to figure out best practices, such as the best way to ship orders, obtain materials, or meet deadlines.

With good planning, smart decisions, and some luck, the business may thrive in those tough early days. Customers might start to phone in new orders. They might also make referrals to their friends, expanding the network of contacts the business relies on. Word-of-mouth referrals are powerful for any business. "People are more inclined to believe something when they hear about it from a trusted source," points out Ivan Estrada in his business book *Brand with Purpose*. "It sticks better than an anonymous broadcast through advertising."[17]

> **"People are more inclined to believe something when they hear about it from a trusted source."[17]**
>
> —Ivan Estrada, author of *Branding with Purpose*

A good Yelp or Google review or a mention in the local newspaper can result in a wave of new business. In the meantime, the owner has to carry out some important tasks in marketing the company, starting with its brand.

Bringing Out the Brand

An important aspect of any business is branding: the image a business projects to its market. The business conveys this image through its advertising, its appearance, and the style of its products. This is also where a good social media strategy can help a business get its message out to a big market of potential customers.

Branding strategies rely on color, fonts, logos, a memorable name, and consistent design. Successful entrepreneurs think carefully about these things. They use the brand to appeal to the market they believe is the right one for whatever they're selling.

Major companies all have a brand. Apple, for instance, brands itself as a sleek, hip consumer tech company whose products appeal to teens and young adults. Branding helps potential customers become familiar with the company—and people tend to trust things that are familiar to them.

Branding also helps a new business solve an important problem: how to get noticed. Although some businesses truly break new ground, most offer familiar products or services. That means they have to stand out somehow and get noticed—which is what good branding will do.

Joining the Lists

Along with developing a brand, entrepreneurs trying to get noticed have to get as many people as possible to see the name of their company. One way to go about this is to set up simple business listings on as many platforms as possible.

Google and Yelp are two of the best-known platforms that offer free business listings. On Google, the listings include name, physical address, phone, business hours, and website links. A business can also add product descriptions and user reviews. Listings on Google are like launch pads. Entrepreneurs use them to build online ad and marketing strategies. On Yelp, users can leave reviews of products and services.

Taking On Partners

It is not uncommon for busy owners of young businesses to reach a point when they feel overwhelmed. This happens when owners make too many commitments, which is an easy thing to do. They then discover that meeting the promises is going to take more

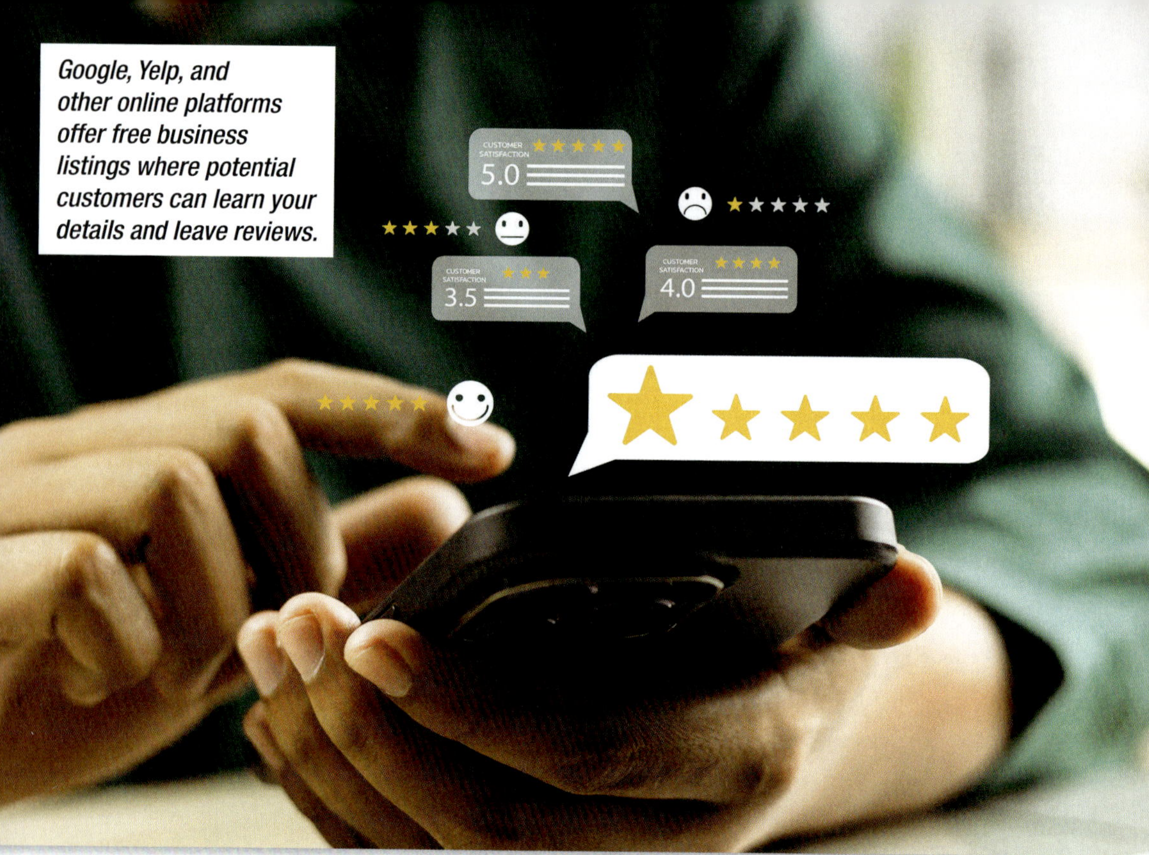

Google, Yelp, and other online platforms offer free business listings where potential customers can learn your details and leave reviews.

time—or skill—than they have. "It is okay to say 'uncle' every now and then and pull in some outside troops to help carry the load," advises Chris Vanderzyden. "We cannot be successful without outside help."[18]

Outside help comes in many forms. Nonprofit organizations may offer mentors, classes or other forms of guidance. An accountant may suggest ways to improve cash flow or profitability. Some businesses hire temporary consultants with expertise in a relevant field. Some overwhelmed business owners consider taking on a partner.

A partner, whether silent or active, invests money in the business and in return is entitled to a share of the profits. A silent partner has no responsibility for running things, but may be able to provide expert advice or bring valuable clients or contacts to the business.

Active partners have an active role. They may be given an important position as a manager of the company. They may handle some of the many tasks, both expected and unexpected, that have come up. Any new partner will have to bring aptitude and energy to the business. They should complement the talents of the owner as much as possible. "A general rule of thumb," comments Ryan Moran in his book *12 Months to $1 Million*, is if your partner has the same qualities that you have, then one of you is unnecessary to the business. Both of you need to bring an element to the table. If one of you is the operator, the other needs to be the big thinker."[19]

> **"If your partner has the same qualities that you have, then one of you is unnecessary to the business."[19]**
>
> —Ryan Moran, author of *12 Months to $1 Million*

On top of it all is a personal connection—business partners have to get along through experiences that would test even a close friendship. Many business partnerships eventually break up, but a few hold together and bring new energy to a company. One turned out well enough to create the biggest consumer tech company in history.

Online Platforms

Doing retail used to mean running a shop or selling things through the mail. The internet added a new selling channel: the online platform.

A web platform provides an online portal for businesses of all sizes. Etsy, for example, allows independent sellers to set up their own stores and advertise their goods for sale. Web platforms save a small business the trouble of creating its own online or physical outlet and developing its own base of customers.

There are many other retail platforms, such as Shopify, Mercari, Amazon, Poshmark, and eBay. They're useful for retail businesses that are starting small or don't have a physical location. Platforms allow an established business to boost sales to a national market.

Getting set up on a platform is easy and inexpensive. The business only has to store inventory, set prices, and handle shipping and returns. A platform business can be easily promoted through social media or by email campaigns. But platforms are very popular among retailers. The challenge lies in marketing and in getting your products, whatever they may be, to stand out in a crowded field.

The Apple Story

In 1971, when Steve Wozniak was in his early twenties, he met a high schooler named Steve Jobs at the Homebrew Computer Club in Menlo Park, California. Jobs seemed to know a lot about computers. He was kind of a tech geek, just like Wozniak. He had an idea to make "blue boxes," which would allow people to make free long-distance phone calls. So the two partnered up.

Things worked out well. The two sold two hundred of the devices and made a little money. Working out of a garage, Wozniak then designed a computer prototype and called it the Apple I. He offered it to Hewlett–Packard, a computer maker he had worked for, but the company turned him down. Then Jobs suggested forming a company to manufacture them. Jobs also secured an order for fifty of the machines from a computer store. With little money to invest, the partners sold some personal items to buy the necessary parts and founded the Apple Computer Company in April 1976.

Starting a business can be overwhelming and time-consuming. Having a partner can be a big help.

It turned out that Wozniak and Jobs had very different talents. But they complemented each other perfectly. "If there was any engineering to do, hardware or software, I did it because Steve could do stuff, but he couldn't do it as well as I," Wozniak later told an interviewer. "So never once did he even try. Never did he look at a circuit and suggest anything. I don't want to mess around running a company—my whole life's engineering—so he's on the phone talking to reporters, talking to stores."[20] Wozniak was the techie, dreaming up new and better designs for a personal computer. Jobs was the marketing genius who figured out how to present those machines to the public.

Apple Computer rode the personal computer wave of the 1980s and 1990s. Its Apple and Macintosh models took the world by storm. The two men parted ways in 1985. Wozniak went on to invent useful consumer tech such as the programmable remote. Jobs applied his marketing smarts to Apple, which eventually turned into the biggest consumer tech company in the world.

Grow or Close

Apple thrived in a very tough tech field. Other companies put good personal computers on the market, but Apple didn't stand still. The company got into personal music devices with the iPod, cell phones with the iPhone, and tablet computing with the iPad. Steve Jobs diversified the company, allowing it to compete in new markets.

Businesses large and small, old and new, have to grow or they won't survive. For a small business owner, it's smart to consider the future, even while concentrating on the present. This means offering the market something new or better. This is a problem facing even small, part-time businesses. A teenager, for example, may earn money mowing lawns on weekend afternoons. But when summer ends in many parts of the country, clients no longer need this service. Plus, there are a lot of other teenagers with mowers doing the same thing. The lawn service business is seasonal, and it's competitive. Soon after establishing the business,

Serial Entrepreneurs

Not all entrepreneurs are interested in growing a single business. Serial entrepreneurs, people who start one company after another, seem to love the challenge of starting and launching businesses into the world.

Richard Branson is well known for this talent. He has founded more than forty different companies. He started with Virgin, a mail-order record business. Then he moved on to Virgin Music and Virgin Atlantic, an airline company.

Not all of Branson's companies succeeded. Virgin Clothing, Virgin Cars, and Virgin Cola, for example, were all failures. But instead of discouraging him, the failures motivated him to try harder. Failure, in his view, can be just another ingredient of success. "It's important to pick yourself up, retrace your steps, look at what went wrong, and learn from your mistakes," he wrote. "If you can learn from the experience, you should be able to avoid making the same errors next time. This is the key to bouncing back, and ultimately the secret to success."

Quoted in Jessica Stillman, "Richard Branson: This Is How You Overcome Your Fear of Failure," *Inc.*, November 17, 2015. www.inc.com.

the owner should already be thinking ahead. The lawn-mowing business might expand to include tree and hedge trimming, landscaping, and snow shoveling. The added service might require the purchase of a truck or other equipment.

The same might be true of a talented cook who launches a home-based catering business. The business owner can set up a small kitchen, grab some clients for parties or weddings, source ingredients from restaurant wholesalers, and serve a nice selection of food from a single table to a hungry crowd. But as the business grows, it will face challenges. It may have too many engagements. It may need a larger kitchen. It might need to add new items to its menu. Thinking ahead means being prepared for eventually hiring servers or other cooks, finding a larger kitchen, or buying new equipment such as ovens or mixers.

Standing still in business is not an option. If the teenage mower or the caterer doesn't take action, the money will stop coming in. As their businesses grow, they will also need to spend time seeking out new customers.

When Challenges Arise

No matter how carefully new business owners plan and prepare, unplanned events and surprises happen. There will always be problems to solve. Some of these problems are minor annoyances that are easy to work out. Others may challenge the new company's survival. Costs may be running too high, or customers may not be paying their bills. For the lawn company, a dry summer means the grass isn't growing and doesn't need mowing.

Another serious issue is profit margin. To be competitive with established businesses that offer similar products or services, a new company might have to charge a lower price. But doing that might not provide a margin of profit. If, for example, it costs the same or more to make cookies than the cookies earn, then a cookie business will lose money. The profit margin isn't big enough, and cash flow is negative. Expenses exceed income, and unless the business owner can right this situation, the business will eventually have to close.

Businesses must be able to grow in order to meet their customers' needs. A lawn-mowing business, for example, could add landscaping services to its offerings.

Customer returns can be another problem. The return policy may allow buyers to return their items within a certain time. Often, this deadline is set to thirty days. This encourages people to buy. But returns may pile up if the product is not meeting expectations. There may be a flaw in the design, or the product may not perform as promised. The business owner has to fix any such issues quickly, or inventory will sit unsold.

Rising inventories is another bad sign for any business, large or small. It's important to have enough of whatever you're selling to meet demand. But when products start to crowd the warehouse, then sales and production aren't in sync. There's either too much production, not enough sales, or too many returns. The market may be rejecting the product or favoring the competition. The situation has to be addressed, and the sooner the better. That's why it's smart for any business to carefully watch inventory levels. They're an excellent sign of the overall health of the business.

Running a business means meeting these and many other challenges. Some of these issues you can anticipate, and some you can't. Solving a business problem—whether it's brought on by competition, product design, or marketing—is just part of the process of starting and running a new business. It makes the business stronger. It gives the owner personal satisfaction and a sense of confidence that no matter what, the business will survive.

CHAPTER FIVE

Starter Stories

It's not necessary to come up with a new business model to start a successful business. As an entrepreneur, your job is to find the model that works best for the business you have in mind. Chances are good that this best model has already been tried many times. In fact, there may be someone already running a similar business in the same market.

According to the US Census Bureau, the United States had a grand total of 5.21 million new business applications in 2024. That many people filed for a license or a permit to operate a new business or registered their business with their state or local government. About one out of every five new businesses fail within a year. In the span of five years, the failure rate goes up to 50 percent.

That's a high rate of failure, but it doesn't seem to discourage young entrepreneurs. The rate of new business registrations has been rising steadily. In fact, registrations are up by about 50 percent since 2020, when many businesses closed their doors during the COVID-19 pandemic. Running a company, big or small, has become something many young people think they can handle. And many who have finished their schooling intend to run their own business rather than work for somebody else. They're not discouraged by the prospect of long hours, low or no pay (at least for a while), and the high stress that comes with business ownership.

Solving the Nanny Problem

Before a business starts, the idea for it arrives. One common way for a business to get going is when someone faces a problem. For Noa Mintz of New York City, the problem was babysitters. She just wasn't happy with the ones her parents hired.

Noa's mother explained that finding a babysitter wasn't easy, even in a big and crowded city. Maybe Noa could do better? Noa accepted the challenge—and met it. She found herself an excellent babysitter. Then she started finding them for friends.

Eventually, her skill in seeking out qualified and experienced caregivers resulted in a business: Nannies by Noa. It was a babysitting agency, set up online, that matched busy parents with quality people for nanny and babysitting jobs. But when Noa started high school, she found that she just didn't have the time necessary to run the business.

She didn't give up. She took on a partner—an adult chief executive officer to take on some of the many tasks involved in running the business. Eventually, the business gained more than two hundred clients, and Nannies by Noa is still going strong. The company has a staff of full-time administrators and has been

Finding good childcare can be difficult. One young entrepreneur identified this problem, and using the skills she already had, found a solution by starting her own business.

covered by *The New York Times*, CNN Money, *Fortune*, *Entrepreneur*, and other top media outlets.

While still in middle school, Noa discovered that she had a talent. She may never have known about it if she hadn't encountered a problem that needed solving. Entrepreneurs often start out this way: They see a problem, and using the skills they already possess, they look for a solution.

Taking the Plunge

On the other side of the world, in Australia, Dominic May was seeing not a problem, but an opportunity. He matched it to his own skills and to his happy place: in or under the water. He was an experienced marine diver and scuba instructor. He loved nothing more than exploring Australia's wild coasts and offshore reefs. It was more than a hobby or a sport. It was a passion, and one that offered a niche for a successful business in marine tourism. In 2018 he dived right in and founded CoastXP.

> **"Constantly comparing yourself to others isn't healthy."[21]**
>
> —Dominic May, CoastXP founder

May realized that travel can be much more than hotels, resorts, and restaurants. There are many interesting experiences that await tourists outside of the usual travel routines. A creative travel company, for example, can draw on local history, exploration in the wild, challenging athletics, cultural experiences such as language or cooking, or protection of the natural environment. CoastXP became one such niche tourism business, and one that perfectly suited May.

Based in Newcastle, Australia, the company offers marine adventures. Participants learn about the local history, geology, and natural environment. The participants board fast boats to encounter marine life and enjoy offshore trips and guided tours.

May has learned a lot about business along the way. He reports that the best advice he ever got was to not compare his business with anybody else's. "It's important to continue to strive to have the best possible experience or product you can, (but) constantly comparing yourself to others isn't healthy,"[21] he says.

AI to the Rescue

Coming up with a marketing plan or ad campaign can take time and money. To overcome this issue, some entrepreneurs are joining the AI wave. They're letting a computer do some of the work.

AI is software that answers queries in natural language. A user types a simple question or request into an AI platform, such as ChatGPT, and gets an answer. Using further prompts, the program can then build a more detailed response.

An AI-generated campaign can suggest ad copy, list different ad channels for a promotion, and help a business rank higher on Google and other search programs. "These days, with a few handy tools like ChatGPT or Claude AI," explain authors Dan S. Kennedy and Parthiv Shah in *Entrepreneur: Startups*, "you can quickly create a highly effective, standout promotional campaign targeted expressly to the audience you want to reach—no need for a marketing team."

Dan S. Kennedy and Parthiv Shah, "AI Made His Marketing. He Made 70K on the Promotion," *Entrepreneur: Startups*, Summer 2025, p. 22.

May and Noa both translated their skills and interests into business start-ups. Their time and energy contributed to the success of their companies. Another very important ingredient is mentorship. The help of an experienced advisor can guide a young entrepreneur over the rough spots. For Jessica Mah, the mentorship aspect of business was key—and she eventually made it into her own valuable business proposition.

Doing It Mah's Way

Jessica Mah found out about Y Combinator when she was nineteen. She had already founded inDinero and many other companies—it was a talent she had been practicing since middle school. Her first business provided server hosting. The business survived, but over the years she had some issues: lack of time, lack of organization, and lack of sleep. Finding a balance in her life was tough.

In search of guidance, she came across Y Combinator. "We help founders at their earliest stages regardless of their age,"[22] declares this start-up accelerator on its home page. The organization assigns a mentor to each founder. The mentor goes through all the important steps in getting the business up and running and helps the start-up raise funds from venture capital investors.

> **"I wish someone told me not to ever get arrogant or cocky with early success."[23]**
>
> —Jessica Mah, Mahway founder

Inspired, Jessica started her own venture capital firm, calling it Mahway. With this, she tries to pass along some wisdom she's picked up on the way to success. "I wish someone told me not to ever get arrogant or cocky with early success. I got caught up in the early press that both my company and I received. Needless to say, the hype did not last for long and I learned a very valuable lesson."[23]

Mah discovered that success can bring overconfidence. An entrepreneur may invest in expanding the business before it's ready. The market may not be ready, and the products may face tough competition. Smart entrepreneurs expand carefully. One way is to try a limited venue such as a street market or a fair. This is how Sweet Martha's grew from a little wooden stand into a chocolate chip cookie empire.

For ocean lovers, a dive boat business might be a way to make a living and have fun at the same time.

The Winning Cookies

Martha Olson ran a frozen yogurt shop in Minneapolis, Minnesota, in the 1970s. Then she dared to dream. She applied for a stand at the Minnesota State Fair. The fair was hosting more than 1 million visitors over twelve days. Fairgoers are a captive market—if they're wandering the grounds and feel hungry for frozen yogurt, for example, they have nowhere else to go.

As a result, the profits for a successful stand at the fair can be huge. But Olson got turned down because the fair already had a yogurt stand. She applied again the next year and the next, and she was turned down both times. So, in 1979 she switched to freshly made chocolate chip cookies. This time, the fair said yes. Her persistence had paid off, but now she had three weeks to come up with a cookie recipe, buy equipment, and build a stand measuring 9 by 11 feet (2.7 by 3.4 m).

Eventually, she solved these problems. Sweet Martha's returned every year, growing sales and becoming a familiar sight to fairgoers. By 2024 Olson's ovens were churning out 3 million

Martha Olson got turned down three years in a row before she was finally accepted as a vendor at the Minnesota State Fair. Today, her Sweet Martha's Cookie Jar booth is a top-selling fixture at the fair.

Brand Protection

Trademarks and intellectual property can be a worry for business owners. If your product or brand is similar to someone else's, there can be a legal issue. That is why you can't name your restaurant McDonald's or make a small, metal toy car called Hot Wheels. When they discover your name and your product, the owners of those trademarks will threaten to sue.

Also, your own products may be copied by someone else. If a business owner comes up with a unique phrase or logo to represent the business, it's smart to register that trademark with the US Patent and Trademark Office. As long as the trademark is registered, nobody can imitate or steal it.

cookies *a day*. The stand's revenue over the fair's twelve days was almost $5 million. That's more than the next three vendors at the fair combined, and more product than the average McDonald's franchise sells in a year.

For Olson and other entrepreneurs, there are always hurdles to overcome. Some problems are minor and can be solved easily. Others, such as Olson's application for a food stand at the Minnesota State Fair, take persistence and sometimes a change of plan. For Lily Born, product design proved to be the roadblock on the route to success. Just getting the shape of a simple drinking mug right was all she needed to create a successful business. She finally reached that goal, but it took years.

Tippy Cups

Lily's grandpa had Parkinson's, a disease that causes the hands to shake. He often had trouble with cups. Coffee, water, and juice would spill across tabletops and sometimes threaten to damage phones and laptop computers. Lily decided to come up with an answer.

Her challenge was to design a cup that wouldn't tip. She added a set of handles or legs to an ordinary mug. The handles would help support the cup so that even a pair of shaking hands wouldn't cause a spill. She brought the design to a clay modeling studio.

It didn't work—the cup still spilled. She changed the length and position of the legs. She changed the number of legs and the angle they formed with the table. Her product development continued for years. Eventually, she hit on a three-legged design that worked. Not only did it work for her grandpa, it also worked for other disabled people and for young children who had problems holding their cups steady.

Lily called her invention the Kangaroo Cup. When she was ten, she started a company with her dad and called it Imagiroo. The company was set up to handle production and marketing of the Kangaroo Cup. For funding, the company turned to Kickstarter, a crowdfunding platform that allows people to invest in start-up companies. The cup was made with many different designs, colors, and materials, and it found acceptance all over the world. After a few years of trial and error, she was on her way.

Lily had learned at least one good lesson. "Starting a business isn't like school," she told an interviewer. "It's almost like you get F's for months and months and then one day your idea works and it's the first time you get a passing grade."[24] The idea of failure and the fear of not living up to expectations stops many people from starting their own business. Failure is just a part of the ordinary start-up business project. It doesn't stop the natural entrepreneur. For some, it can contribute to eventual success.

SOURCE NOTES

Introduction: What It Takes to Start a Business

1. Quoted in *Entrepreneur*, "Dan Lok Failed in 13 Business Ventures over 3 Years. Now This Unemployable Immigrant Manages Millions and Mentors Young Entrepreneurs," July 16, 2019. www.entrepreneur.com.
2. Jesse Kemmerer, "Advice from a Young Entrepreneur Who (Mostly) Failed," Young Upstarts, September 5, 2022. www.youngupstarts.com.
3. Kemmerer, "Advice from a Young Entrepreneur Who (Mostly) Failed."

Chapter One: Just Starting Out

4. Quoted in Mike Winters, "Early Retiree Flipped a House, Launched a Company and Sold It for $12.5 Million—All Before Turning 30," CNBC, May 22, 2025. www.cnbc.com.
5. Quoted in Nicole Fallon-Peek, "10 Successful Young Entrepreneurs," Investopedia, April 15, 2025. www.investopedia.com.
6. Quoted in Wil Chan, "11 Best Business Networking Groups for New Businesses," Next Insurance, January 2, 2025. www.nextinsurance.com.
7. Jake Butler, *Teen Entrepreneur: The Dream.* 424, 2024, p. 7.
8. Quoted in Jazlynn Trinidade, "Interview with Young Entrepreneur Rayhan: The Vision Behind Snacc," *Youth Incorporated*, May 12, 2025. https://youthincmag.com.

Chapter Two: Making a Plan

9. Chris Vanderzyden, *A–Z Blueprint for Success.* Balboa, 2012, p. 3.
10. Quoted in Zara Stone, "11 Times Mark Zuckerberg Kept It Real," *Forbes*, October 11, 2016. www.forbes.com.
11. Quoted in Alessio Bresciani, "51 Mission Statement Examples from the World's Best Companies." https://alessiobresciani.com.
12. Quoted in JMax Plumbing, "Q&A with Bunim Laskin, Founder and CEO of Swimply: The Airbnb of Pools," August 22, 2024. https://jmaxplumbing.com.

Chapter Three: Getting to Opening Day

13. Quoted in Dignity of Children, "Inspiring Young Entrepreneurs: An Interview with Brian Weisfeld, Founder, the Startup Squad," March 22, 2023. www.dignityofchildren.com.
14. Dayna Winter, "14 Creative Grand Opening Ideas for Every Business in 2024," Shopify, January 8, 2024. www.shopify.com.
15. Allan Dib, *The 1-Page Marketing Plan.* Page Two, 2023, p. 22.
16. Quoted in "StudyFetch: Transforming Education with Pioneering AI-Enhanced Learning Solutions and IP Security," Education Technology Insights, 2025. www.educationtechnologyinsights.com.

Chapter Four: After the Doors Open

17. Ivan Estrada, *Brand with Purpose.* Page Two, 2021, p. 195.
18. Vanderzyden, *A–Z Blueprint for Success*, p. 13.
19. Ryan Moran, *12 Months to $1 Million*. BenBella, 2020, p. xxxvi.
20. Quoted in Founders at Work, "Interview: Steve Wozniak." www.foundersatwork.com.

Chapter Five: Starter Stories

21. Quoted in Madelaine Love, "6 Young Entrepreneurs Making Waves," Hippocampus, May 2, 2023. www.newcastle.edu.au.
22. Y Combinator, home page, 2025. www.ycombinator.com.
23. Quoted in Y Combinator, "Female Founder Stories: Jessica Mah," 2025. www.femalefounderstories.com.
24. Quoted in Ellie McRae, "Interview with Lily Born," Kebloom, December 10, 2018. www.kebloom.com.

INTERVIEW WITH A NEW BUSINESS CREATOR

LaShanda Brittian started Kaukau Bento in 2024 in San Diego, California. Kaukau Bento is a food business focused on crafting high-quality, freshly prepared meals that go directly from the kitchen to refrigerated vending machines. These machines are designed to be placed in businesses, schools, and other high-traffic locations, offering the convenience of fully prepared meals available around the clock. She answered questions about the process of starting her new business by email.

Q: Why did you decide to start your own business?
A: After more than 20 years in the software industry, I unexpectedly lost my job. It was a moment of uncertainty but also a turning point. I had always dreamed of being my own boss, and this gave me the push I needed. Instead of returning to what I'd always done, I took a step back and asked myself what I truly enjoyed—and for me, that was cooking. I decided to take a leap of faith and start a food business, even though I knew it would be challenging. The idea of creating something from scratch, something meaningful and completely my own, gave me the inspiration to move forward.

Q: How did you decide what kind of business to start?
A: Once I realized I wanted to reinvent myself, I looked at the skills and passions I already had. I've always loved to cook and share food with others, and I saw a need for convenient, high-quality meals—especially for busy people on tight schedules. That's when the concept for Kaukau Bento came together. I used what I knew, stayed open to learning along the way, and made a plan to build a business that combined my creativity, my work ethic, and my passion for food. It wasn't an easy decision, but it was a purposeful one.

Q: What kind of planning or preparation did you do before getting started?
A: Since I had never started a business before, I honestly didn't know where to begin. I had always worked for companies, so stepping into entrepreneurship was completely new to me. That meant I had to learn everything from the ground up. One of the most helpful resources I

found was SCORE San Diego, a nonprofit that offers mentorship and business classes for small business owners. Through SCORE, I was paired with a mentor and attended as many workshops as I could—many of which were free or low-cost. They offered classes on topics like writing a business plan, understanding taxes, and navigating the basics of launching a business.

Another resource I used was the Small Business Administration (SBA). Like SCORE, the SBA provides valuable support for small business owners, including mentorship and educational programs.

In addition to general business planning, I had to prepare specifically for starting a food business. I began by designing a menu that reflected my heritage—I'm from Hawaii, and I wanted my food to represent where I come from. I also had a unique idea: I wanted to place my meals in refrigerated vending machines that also had heating capabilities. So I researched manufacturers that create machines with both refrigeration and built-in microwaves, which took a lot of time and effort to understand what would work best for my vision.

Finally, there were all the legal and regulatory steps. I researched what kind of business entity I wanted—ultimately choosing an LLC—and then applied for a business license, seller's permit, and health permits to legally operate a food business in California.

There's a lot of planning that goes into launching any business, but my advice is to start with what you don't know, ask questions, use your local resources, and build up your knowledge one step at a time.

Q: Which of those things did you find most valuable?

A: It's hard to choose just one, because every part of the preparation process played an important role in helping me launch my business. But if I had to pick the most valuable, it would be the mentorship and support I received through SCORE and the SBA.

While the workshops and classes were incredibly informative, what made the biggest difference for me was having someone to talk to—someone who had experience starting and running a business, and who could offer guidance specific to my situation. Being able to ask questions, get honest feedback, and simply talk through challenges with a mentor gave me the confidence to move forward. Starting a business can feel overwhelming, especially when you're doing it for the first time. Having that one-on-one connection with someone who had walked the path before made a huge difference in helping me believe I could do it, too.

Q: Is there anything you wish you had researched or thought more about before starting your business?

A: Before launching my business, I had a general idea of who I thought my target market would be. My goal was to provide fresh meals through refrigerated vending machines, which are accessible 24/7—so naturally, I thought warehouses would be the perfect place to start. I imagined young, hungry workers—mostly men between the ages of 18 and 35—who needed quick, hot meals during any shift.

While the concept made sense in theory, I now realize I should have spent more time doing on-the-ground research—actually visiting warehouses, speaking with workers and managers, and learning more about their eating habits, break times, and preferences. If I'd had even six months to a year to fully research and engage with that audience, I think I would've made more informed decisions early on.

That said, entrepreneurship is often about pivoting—learning from real-world experience and adjusting as you go. What surprised me is that my original target audience (young men, 18 to 35) was still accurate—but the military community, not warehouse workers, turned out to be a better fit for my product. I now do a pop-up lunch service outside of a Navy base, and I've found that this audience not only appreciates the food, but also responds well to my pricing and value.

It's a great reminder that you can't always predict how things will turn out. You have to stay open-minded, do as much research as you can—and then be flexible and ready to adapt when reality teaches you something new.

Q: What has been the most difficult part of starting your own business?

A: For me, the most difficult part was getting people to say yes to something new—specifically, my food and the vending machine concept. It's not just about having a great product; it's about getting others to believe in it, too. I probably heard a hundred no's before I got my first real yes.

One of the biggest challenges was simply getting to the right person—the actual decision maker. I knocked on doors, handed out business cards, followed up with emails, and returned multiple times to try to make connections. But more often than not, I ran into gatekeepers—people who were friendly but couldn't make any decisions. It was frustrating and exhausting, especially when I believed in what I was offering.

That experience taught me a lot about resilience and the importance of persistence. If you're starting something new, especially something innovative or unfamiliar, you have to be ready for rejection and still keep going. Eventually, someone will say yes—but you have to be willing to push through all the no's to find them.

Q: What has been the most exciting part of starting your own business?

A: The most exciting part has been the sense of pride and ownership that comes from building something entirely my own. Starting a business is a big responsibility—every decision, every success, every mistake is on me—but that's also what makes it so fulfilling. I get to shape my business around what I believe in and what I care about.

It's especially exciting to see people truly enjoy the food I make. When customers come back and tell me how much they love it—sometimes over and over again—it reminds me that I'm on the right path. It gives me that extra reassurance that all the hard work, all the planning, and all the long hours are worth it. Knowing that something I created is bringing joy to others is one of the best feelings in the world.

Q: What traits and skills do you think are important to be successful in starting your own business?

A: The first word that comes to mind is *grit*. Starting a business takes real determination. You'll face long hours, rejection, and obstacles you never saw coming. You have to push through all of it with a deep belief in what you're doing—even when others don't see the vision yet.

You also need mental and physical stamina. Some days are draining, both emotionally and physically, especially if you're doing everything yourself. But that persistence pays off.

Another important trait is resourcefulness. When I didn't know where to start, I sought out help from SCORE and the SBA, attended workshops, found mentors, and did the research I needed to move forward.

You also need to be flexible and willing to pivot. What you imagine in the beginning may not turn out exactly how things go. That doesn't mean you've failed—it means you're learning. I originally planned to focus on warehouse workers, but I found my strongest customer base among military personnel. Being open to those shifts is crucial.

Finally, it helps to have creativity and passion—especially if your business is personal to you, like mine is. I created Kaukau Bento to reflect where I'm from and what I love. That sense of purpose helps carry you through the tough moments and makes the wins even more meaningful.

Q: What advice do you have for teens who might want to someday start a business of their own?

A: The most important advice I can give is this: believe in yourself and believe in your product. Whatever your idea is—whether it's a food item, a service, or something brand new—you have to believe in it 100%. If you don't believe in it, no one else will.

Starting a business is like planting a seed. You have to nurture it, give it attention, patience, and time to grow. There will be days when things don't go as planned, and that's when your belief in yourself becomes even more important.

Also, trust yourself. Trust your vision, your instincts, and your ability to learn along the way. And whatever you do, don't give up. Keep going. Keep pushing. Keep learning. Keep showing up. Success doesn't usually come quickly—but if you stay committed and believe in what you're building, it will come.

FOR FURTHER RESEARCH

Books

Jake Butler, *Teen Entrepreneur: The Dream*. Published by author, 2024.

Leanne Currie-McGhee, *How Do I Start a Business?*," San Diego, CA: ReferencePoint, 2024.

Mike Hogan, *Teen Entrepreneur: Be Part of the New Rich and Become a Teen Million/Billionaire Entrepreneur in Today's Worldwide Economy*. MM Publishing, 2023.

Annika Launay and Briana Cicchello, *Entrepreneur for Teens: The Ultimate Guide to Your Future Career*. Published by the author, 2024.

Brian Weisfeld, *The Startup Squad: You're the Boss. A Kid's Ultimate Guide to Starting Your Own Business*. Philomel, 2024.

Internet Sources

Lydia DePillis, "Under Trump, a Mainstay for Small Businesses Clamps Down," *New York Times*, May 23, 2025. www.nytimes.com.

Forbes Business Council, "Starting a Business? 20 Steps to Catapult Success," *Forbes*, May 29, 2025. www.forbes.com.

Miranda Fraraccio, "19 Free Resources for Small Businesses to Leverage Year-Round," CO—, April 21, 2025. www.uschamber.com.

Joshua Stowers, "How to Start a Business: A Step-by-Step Guide," Business News Daily, February 4, 2025. www.businessnewsdaily.com.

Robin Waite, "Essential Steps for Setting Business Every Young Entrepreneur Should Know," *The Fearless Business Blog*, November 18, 2024. www.robinwaite.com/blog/essential-steps-for-setting-business-every-young-entrepreneur-should-know.

Websites

Google for Startups

https://startup.google.com

On this site the big search engine links to its resources for small companies, including financial and promotional tools. Some are free, while others require an investment or subscription fee.

Grants.gov
https://grants.gov
A government directory of all the federal agencies offering business grants, including grants to small and start-up businesses. The site assists users in filing applications and tracking them through the system.

NerdWallet
www.nerdwallet.com/h/category/small-business
This site offers useful financial tools and information for small business and new business owners. Featured topics include business loans, business bank accounts, and business software. Also on the site are articles outlining how to start a business and how to write a business plan.

SCORE
www.score.org
A national nonprofit organization designed to help small businesses still in the idea stage succeed. Through local offices, the group offers one-on-one coaching by experienced volunteers, as well as online resources, success stories, meetings, and seminars that can help start-ups get successfully launched.

Small Business Administration (SBA)
www.sba.gov
The SBA is a federal agency set up to assist business owners with low-interest loans and other resources. Its website includes resources for planning, launching, managing, and growing new businesses.

Wave
www.waveapps.com
A site that offers free, simple accounting tools as well as premium (paid) levels. Small business owners can create invoices, accept payments, keep track of their bank account, deal with taxes, and measure their financial health with graphs of important metrics, such as sales revenue and cash flow.

Wefunder
https://wefunder.com
A crowdfunding site that links businesses with private investors. Once it's ready to launch, a start-up business would create a listing describing its products/services, management, and market, and interested supporters have the opportunity to kick in funds in return for a stake in the company's future profits. Similar sites include Kickstarter, Start-Engine, and Fundable.

INDEX

Note: Boldface page numbers indicate illustrations.

PICTURE CREDITS

Cover: Shutterstock.com

5: Monkey Business Images/Shutterstock
10: f.t.Photographer/Shutterstock
13: Ground Picture/Shutterstock
15: Monkey Business Images/Shutterstock
17: Frederic Legrand – COMEO/Shutterstock
21: Meeko Media/Shutterstock
23: Mikeledray/Shutterstock
26: Antoniodiaz/Shutterstock
29: Prostock-studio/Shutterstock
32: Chay_Tee/Shutterstock
36: GamePixel/Shutterstock
38: Ground Picture/Shutterstock
41: Virrage Images/Shutterstock
44: Media Photos/Shutterstock
47: Richard Whitcombe/Shutterstock
48: Gina Kelly/Shutterstock

ABOUT THE AUTHOR

Tom Streissguth has been writing nonfiction and reference books for schools and libraries for more than thirty years. He graduated with a degree in music from Yale University and has worked as a teacher and editor. In 2015 he founded The Archive, an online collection of historic journalism by American authors. He lives in the Twin Cities area, where he grew up, and has three daughters.